Pope Benedict XVI on Vatican Council II

50th Anniversary of the Second Vatican Council

by
Pope Benedict XVI
Ed. Lucio Coco

*All booklets are published thanks to the
generous support of the members of the
Catholic Truth Society*

CATHOLIC TRUTH SOCIETY

PUBLISHERS TO THE HOLY SEE

Contents

All rights reserved. First published 2013 by The Incorporated Catholic Truth Society, 40-46 Harleyford Road London SE11 5AY Tel: 020 7640 0042 Fax: 020 7640 0046. Translated from the original Italian publication: Pensieri sulla Fede. *Copyright © Libreria Editrice Vaticana, Citta del Vaticano. This edition © The Incorporated Catholic Truth Society 2013.*

ISBN 978 1 86082 840 9

Introduction

"As I prepare myself for the service that is proper to the Successor of Peter, I also wish to confirm my determination to continue to put the Second Vatican Council into practice, following in the footsteps of my Predecessors and in faithful continuity with the 2,000-year tradition of the Church." These were among the first words spoken by Pope Benedict XVI in his Mass together with the Cardinal electors soon after his election to the pontificate (*Speech*, 20.4.05). He went on to add "...this very year marks the 40th anniversary of the conclusion of the Council (8 December 1965). As the years have passed, the Conciliar Documents have lost none of their timeliness; indeed, their teachings are proving particularly relevant to the new situation of the Church and the current globalised society."

Benedict XVI's pontificate has been providentially marked by two anniversaries, the 40th anniversary of the conclusion of Vatican II in the year of his election, and the 50th anniversary of the beginning of the Council, which the Holy Father has chosen to commemorate with a Year of Faith beginning on 11 October 2012, which coincides with the date of the first meeting of the Second Vatican Council. The real significance of this date is outlined in the Pope's letter *Porta Fidei*: "It seemed to me that timing the launch of the Year of Faith to coincide with the fiftieth anniversary of the opening of the Second Vatican Council would provide a good opportunity to help people understand that the texts bequeathed by the Council Fathers, in the words of Blessed John Paul II, *'have lost nothing of their value or brilliance'* (*Novo Millennio Ineunte*)" (*Porta Fidei*, 5).

Pope Benedict XVI himself is utterly convinced of the importance and relevance of this ecclesial event, so much so that soon after his election he felt able to say: "it can be and can become increasingly powerful for the ever-necessary renewal of the Church" (*Speech*, 22.12.05). The task which the Council set itself was to express the truth of Christ in a new way to modern man. The whole Council was inspired by the wish to communicate Christ the Light of the world to contemporary man. (*Cf. Paul VI Speech*, 29 September 1963.) Looking back on the time of the Council, Pope Benedict remarked that from the heart of the Church "emerged the impelling desire, awakened by the Spirit, *for a new epiphany of Christ in the world*" (*Homily*, 6.1.07) - a world which had been radically changed by modern times and which no longer corresponded to outmoded and narrow Eurocentric or western perspectives. It was necessary to build up a new vision, not only in economics and politics but also in culture and in spiritual spheres, which was capable of interpreting the new dynamics that the modern world threw up.

Vatican II set out to describe a Church that was on a journey, that was able to look at herself and her constituent elements, her hierarchy, liturgy, and the centrality of Sacred Scripture, and to offer the results of this effort of self-understanding to the world around her in which she is immersed, but to which at the same time she must bring the living leaven of Christ.

From this perspective, Pope Benedict recognised the great pastoral wisdom of his predecessors who "steered the boat of Peter on the course of authentic conciliar renewal, ceaselessly working for the faithful interpretation and implementation of Vatican Council II" (*Angelus*, 8.12.05). We can undoubtedly say the same of Pope Benedict's own actions. He has, during the entire course of his pontificate welcomed the fundamental recommendations of the Council and been a tireless advocate of the Missionary Church who brings Christ to all men and commits herself to make salvation available to the whole of humanity.

The reading of the Council proposed by Benedict XVI is always one of continuity with the past. In his speech to the Roman Curia of 22 December 2005, at the very beginning of his magisterium, the Holy Father insisted on the necessity of rejecting an approach based on discontinuity. When approaching the salient themes of the Council he preferred instead "the hermeneutic of reform", of "innovation in continuity", which is the only interpretation that allows the good seed of faith which was sown at the time to grow and continue to develop. A significant portion of this important speech has been reproduced in this booklet. In the same way, all the texts offered in this booklet present ample evidence of the Holy Father's efforts in indicating a thread of continuity between the post-conciliar Church and the Church throughout the ages. In that same speech Pope Benedict affirmed that "the Church, both before and after the Council, was and is the same Church, one, holy, catholic and apostolic, journeying on through time; she continues 'her pilgrimage amid the persecutions of the world and the consolations of God' (St Augustine, *De civitate Dei*, XVII, 51,2: PL 41, 614), proclaiming the death of the Lord until he comes (cf. *Lumen Gentium*, n. 8)."

In this perspective Pope Benedict continually recalls the Conciliar documents to once again give to the Church that universal and prophetic breath which the Council had given her in reflecting on her own nature and constitution, that of being "the mystical body of Christ" (*Lumen Gentium*, 7). It is Christ in fact who renders the Council relevant even now: without his lifegiving influence, how could the Council's decisions and documents speak to us even today? It is Christ who comes to give life to the written words which otherwise would remain indecipherable and inapplicable to the urgent necessities which life imposes on modern man. Remembering the years of Vatican II, the Holy Father said the following, which can be considered almost the seal and summary of that vital experience in the life of the Church: "In these past 60 years, almost everything has changed, but the Lord's fidelity has remained. He is the same yesterday, today and for ever: and this is our certainty that paves our way to the future. The moment of memory, the moment of gratitude is also the moment of hope: *In te Domine speravi, non confundar in aeternum* [In you, O Lord, have I hoped, let me never be confounded)]" (*Speech*, 1.7.11).

Lucio Coco

Every Council is born from the Church and returns to the Church.

Benedict XVI

If we interpret and implement the Council guided by a right hermeneutic, it can be and can become increasingly powerful for the ever-necessary renewal of the Church.

Benedict XVI

The Hermeneutic of the Council

What has been the result of the Council? Was it well received? What, in the acceptance of the Council, was good and what was inadequate or mistaken? What still remains to be done? No one can deny that in vast areas of the Church the implementation of the Council has been somewhat difficult, even without wishing to apply to what occurred in these years the description that St Basil, the great Doctor of the Church, made of the Church's situation after the Council of Nicea: he compares her situation to a naval battle in the darkness of the storm, saying among other things: "The raucous shouting of those who through disagreement rise up against one another, the incomprehensible chatter, the confused din of uninterrupted clamouring, has now filled almost the whole of the Church, falsifying through excess or failure the right doctrine of the faith..." (*De Spiritu Sancto*, XXX, 77; *PG* 32, 213 A; SCh 17 ff., p. 524).

We do not want to apply precisely this dramatic description to the situation of the post-conciliar period, yet something from all that occurred is nevertheless reflected in it. The question arises: Why has the implementation of the Council, in large parts of the Church, thus far been so difficult?

Well, it all depends on the correct interpretation of the Council or - as we would say today - on its proper hermeneutics, the correct key to its interpretation and application. The problems in its implementation arose from the fact that two contrary hermeneutics came face to face and quarrelled with each other. One caused confusion, the other, silently but more and more visibly, bore and is bearing fruit.

On the one hand, there is an interpretation that I would call "a hermeneutic of discontinuity and rupture"; it has frequently availed itself of the sympathies of the mass media, and also one trend of modern theology. On the other, there is the "hermeneutic of reform", of renewal in the continuity of the one subject-Church which the Lord has given to us. She is a subject which increases in time and develops, yet always remaining the same, the one subject of the journeying People of God.

The hermeneutic of discontinuity risks ending in a split between the pre-conciliar Church and the post-conciliar Church. It asserts that the texts of the Council as such do not yet express the true spirit of the Council. It claims that they are the result of compromises in which, to reach unanimity, it was found necessary to keep and reconfirm many old things that are now pointless. However, the true spirit of the Council is not to be found in these compromises but instead in the impulses toward the new that are contained in the texts.

These innovations alone were supposed to represent the true spirit of the Council, and starting from and in conformity with them, it would be possible to move ahead. Precisely because the texts would only imperfectly reflect the true spirit of the Council and its newness, it would be necessary to go courageously beyond the texts and make room for the newness in which the Council's deepest intention would be expressed, even if it were still vague.

In a word: it would be necessary not to follow the texts of the Council but its spirit. In this way, obviously, a vast margin was left open for the question on how this spirit should subsequently be defined and room was consequently made for every whim.

The nature of a Council as such is therefore basically misunderstood. In this way, it is considered as a sort of constituent that eliminates an old constitution and creates a new one. However, the Constituent Assembly needs a mandator and then confirmation by the mandator, in other words, the people the constitution must serve. The Fathers had no such mandate and no one had ever given them one; nor could anyone have given them one because the essential constitution of the Church comes from the Lord and was given to us so that we might attain eternal life and, starting from this perspective, be able to illuminate life in time and time itself.

Through the Sacrament they have received, Bishops are stewards of the Lord's gift. They are "stewards of the mysteries of God" (*1 Co* 4:1); as such, they must be found to be "faithful" and "wise" (cf. *Lk* 12:41-48). This requires them to administer the Lord's gift in the right way, so that it is not left concealed in some hiding place but bears fruit, and the Lord may end by saying to the administrator: "Since you were dependable in a small matter I will put you in charge of larger affairs" (cf. *Mt* 25:14-30; *Lk* 19:11-27).

These Gospel parables express the dynamic of fidelity required in the Lord's service; and through them it becomes clear that, as in a Council, the dynamic and fidelity must converge.

The hermeneutic of discontinuity is countered by the hermeneutic of reform, as it was presented first by Pope John XXIII in his Speech inaugurating the Council on 11 October 1962 and later by Pope Paul VI in his Discourse for the Council's conclusion on 7 December 1965.

Here I shall cite only John XXIII's well-known words, which unequivocally express this hermeneutic when he says that the Council wishes "to transmit the doctrine, pure and integral, without any attenuation or distortion". And he continues: "Our duty is not only to guard this precious treasure, as if we were concerned only with antiquity, but to dedicate ourselves with an earnest will and without fear to that work which our era demands of us...". It is necessary that "adherence to all the teaching of the Church in its entirety and preciseness..." be presented in "faithful and perfect conformity to the authentic doctrine, which, however, should be studied and expounded through the methods of research and through the literary forms of modern thought. The substance of the ancient doctrine of the deposit of faith is one thing, and the way in which it is presented is another...", retaining the same meaning and message (*The Documents of Vatican II*, Walter M. Abbott, S.J., p. 715).

It is clear that this commitment to expressing a specific truth in a new way demands new thinking on this truth and a new and vital relationship with it; it is also clear that new words can only develop if they come from an informed understanding of the truth expressed, and on the other hand, that a reflection on faith also requires that this faith be lived. In this regard, the programme that Pope John XXIII proposed was extremely demanding, indeed, just as the synthesis of fidelity and dynamic is demanding.

However, wherever this interpretation guided the implementation of the Council, new life developed and new fruit ripened. Forty years after the Council, we can show that the positive is far greater and livelier than it appeared to be in the turbulent years around 1968. Today, we see that although the good seed developed slowly, it is nonetheless growing; and our deep gratitude for the work done by the Council is likewise growing.

Benedictus PP XVI

Benedict XVI

I. The Compass of the Council

1. Contemporary importance

Therefore, in preparing myself also for the service that is proper to the Successor of Peter, I also wish to affirm strongly my determination to continue the commitment to implement the Second Vatican Council, following in the footsteps of my Predecessors and in faithful continuity with the 2,000-year tradition of the Church.... With the passing of the years, the conciliar documents have not lost their current importance; on the contrary, their teachings reveal themselves particularly pertinent in relation to the new needs of the Church and of the present globalised society.

First Message, 20.4.05

2. Motivations of the Council

The whole of the Second Vatican Council was truly stirred by the longing to proclaim Christ, the Light of the world, to contemporary humanity. In the heart of the Church, from the summit of her hierarchy, emerged the impelling desire, awakened by the Spirit, *for a new epiphany of Christ in the world*, a world that the modern epoch had profoundly transformed and that, for the first time in history, found itself facing the challenge of a global civilisation in which the centre could no longer be Europe or even what we call the West and the North of the world.

The need to work out a new world political and economic order was emerging but, at the same time and above all, one that would be both spiritual and cultural, that is, a renewed humanism.

This observation became more and more obvious: a new world economic and political order cannot work unless there is a spiritual renewal, unless we can once again draw close to God and find God in our midst.

Before the Second Vatican Council, the enlightened minds of Christian thinkers had already intuited and faced this epochal challenge.

Well, at the beginning of the third millennium, we find ourselves in the midst of this phase of human history that now focuses on the word "globalisation".

Homily, 6.1.07

3. Purpose

Precisely so as "to place the modern world in contact with the life-giving and perennial energies of the Gospel" (John XXIII, Apostolic Constitution *Humanae Salutis*, 3), the Second Vatican Council was convened. There the Church, on the basis of a renewed awareness of the Catholic tradition, took seriously and discerned, transformed and overcame the fundamental critiques that gave rise to the modern world, the Reformation and the Enlightenment. In this way the Church herself accepted and refashioned the best of the requirements of modernity by transcending them on the one hand, and on the other by avoiding their errors and dead ends. The Council laid the foundation for an authentic Catholic renewal and for a new civilisation - "the civilisation of love" - as an evangelical service to man and society.

Speech, 12.5.10

4. Continuity

Vatican II embraces the entire doctrinal history of the Church. Anyone who wishes to be obedient to the Council has to accept the faith professed over the centuries, and cannot sever the roots from which the tree draws its life.

Letter, 10.3.09

5. Inheritance (1)

We are all truly indebted to this extraordinary ecclesial event. The multiple doctrinal legacy that we find in its Dogmatic Constitutions, Declarations and Decrees still stimulates us to deepen our knowledge of the Word of God in order to apply it to the Church in the present day, keeping clearly in mind the many needs of the men and women of the contemporary world who are extremely in need of knowing and experiencing the light of Christian hope.

Message, 28.10.08

6. Inheritance (2)

Thus, I think we have to rediscover the Council's great legacy. It is not a spirit reconstructed from texts but consists of the great Council texts themselves, reinterpreted today with the experiences we have had which have borne fruit in so many movements and so many new religious communities.

Speech, 24.6.07

7. Just hermeneutics

If we interpret and implement [the Council] guided by a right hermeneutic, it can be and can become increasingly powerful for the ever-necessary renewal of the Church.

Speech, 22.12.05

II. Constitutions

Sacrosanctum Concilium
**(Constitution on the Sacred Liturgy,
4 December 1963)**

8. Continuity

In the history of the liturgy there is growth and progress,
but no rupture.

Letter, 7.7.07

9. The Tradition of faith

It is necessary above all not to neglect the common Catholic
spirituality which is expressed in the Liturgy and in the great
Tradition of faith. This seems to me to be very important.
This point is also important with regard to the Council.

We need not, … live the hermeneutic of discontinuity, but
rather the hermeneutic of renewal, which is the spirituality
of continuity, of going ahead in continuity. This seems to
me to be very important also as regards the Liturgy.… We
must accept newness but also love continuity, and we must
see the Council in this perspective of continuity. This will
also help us in mediating between the generations in their
way of communicating the faith.

Speech, 2.3.06

10. The figure of Christ

"[The real nature of the true Church...] is essentially both human and divine, visible but endowed with invisible realties, zealous in action and dedicated to contemplation, present in the world, but as a pilgrim, so constituted that in her the human is directed toward and subordinated to the divine, the visible to the invisible, action to contemplation, and this present world to that city yet to come, the object of our quest" (*Sacrosanctum Concilium*, n. 2). If in the Liturgy the figure of Christ who is its principle and is really present to make it effective were not to emerge, we should no longer have the Christian liturgy, completely dependent upon the Lord and sustained by his creative presence.

Speech, 15.4.10

11. Liturgy and prayer

In the first place, it is important for you to take care of the liturgy, which, as the Second Vatican Council teaches: "daily builds up those who are in the Church... into a holy temple of the Lord ... to the mature measure of the fullness of Christ. At the same time it marvellously increases their power to preach Christ" (*Sacrosanctum Concilium*, n. 2).

May an intense life of prayer and assiduous participation in the liturgy continue to be your priority commitment, as individuals and as a sodality.

Speech, 17.6.06

12. Care

The Constitution *Sacrosanctum Concilium* stresses that it is in the Liturgy that the mystery of the Church is made manifest in its grandeur and its simplicity (cf. Introduction, n. 2). Thus it is important that priests take care in liturgical celebrations, particularly the Eucharist, to ensure that they permit a profound communion with the Living God, Father, Son and Holy Spirit. It is necessary that celebrations take place with respect for the Church's liturgical tradition, with the active participation of the faithful, according to each one's specific role, uniting personally with Christ's Paschal Mystery.

Speech, 8.5.10

13. Liturgy, a living reality

There is no opposition between the liturgy renewed by the Second Vatican Council and this liturgy.

On each day [of the Council], the Council Fathers celebrated Mass in accordance with the ancient rite and, at the same time, they conceived of a natural development for the liturgy within the whole of this century, for the liturgy is a living reality that develops but, in its development, retains its identity. Thus, there are certainly different accents, but nevertheless [there remains] a fundamental identity that excludes a contradiction, an opposition between the renewed liturgy and the previous liturgy. In any case, I believe that there is an opportunity for the enrichment of both parties. On the one hand the friends of the old liturgy can and must know the new saints, the new prefaces of the liturgy, etc.... On the other, the new liturgy places greater emphasis on common participation, but it is not merely an assembly of a certain community, but rather always an act of the universal Church in communion with all believers of all times, and an act of worship. In this sense, it seems to me that there is a mutual enrichment, and it is clear that the renewed liturgy is the ordinary liturgy of our time.

Speech, 12.9.08

14. The veneration of images

But then the new step is that this mysterious God liberates us from the inflation of images and from an age filled with images of divinities and gives us the freedom of vision of the essential. God appears with a face, a body, a human history, which is at the same time divine. It is a history that continues in the history of saints, martyrs, saints of charity, of the word, who are always an explanation, a continuation of his divine and human life in the Body of Christ and give us the fundamental images in which - over and above superficial images that conceal reality - we can open our gaze to Truth itself. In this regard I find the iconoclastic period of the post-conciliar years excessive; yet it had a meaning of its own since it may have been necessary to be freed from the superficiality of too many images.

Speech, 7.2.08

15. Liturgical renewal

The liturgical renewal which began with the Second Vatican Ecumenical Council had a beneficial influence on the life of the Church. The Synod of Bishops was able to evaluate the reception of the renewal in the years following the Council. There were many expressions of appreciation. The difficulties and even the occasional abuses which were noted, it was affirmed, cannot overshadow the benefits and the validity of the liturgical renewal, whose riches are yet to be fully explored. Concretely, the changes which the Council called for need to be understood within the overall unity of the historical development of the rite itself, without the introduction of artificial discontinuities.

Sacramentum Caritatis, 3

16. Beyond the reform of the Council

The Liturgy of the Church goes beyond the "conciliar reform" itself (cf. *Sacrosanctum Concilium*, n. 1), whose aim, in fact, was not primarily to change the rites and the texts, but rather to renew mentalities and to put at the centre of Christian life and ministry the celebration of the Paschal Mystery of Christ. Unfortunately, perhaps, we too, Pastors and experts, understood the Liturgy as an *object* to be reformed rather than a *subject* capable of renewing Christian life, since "A very close and organic bond exists between the renewal of the Liturgy and the renewal of the whole life of the Church. The Church not only acts but also expresses herself in the Liturgy and draws from the Liturgy the strength for her life". Blessed John Paul II reminds us of this in *Vicesimus Quintus Annus*, in which the Liturgy is seen *as the vibrant heart of all ecclesial activity*.

Speech, 6.5.11

Lumen Gentium
(Dogmatic Constitution on the Church, 21 November 1964)

17. Intimate union

[We need] to perceive the Church, as she is presented to us by the Second Vatican Council, as a sacrament of intimate union with God, hence, of unity among all of us and, lastly, among the whole human race (cf. *Lumen Gentium*, n. 1).

Catechesis, 12.12.07

18. Mystery of communion

In a society fraught between globalisation and individualism, the Church is called to offer a witness of *koinonìa*, of communion. This reality does not come "from below" but is a mystery which, so to speak, "has its roots in Heaven", in the Triune God himself. It is he, in himself, who is the eternal dialogue of love which was communicated to us in Jesus Christ and woven into the fabric of humanity and history to lead it to fullness. And here then is the great synthesis of the Second Vatican Council: the Church, mystery of communion, "in Christ is in the nature of sacrament - a sign and instrument, that is, of communion with God and of unity among all men" (Dogmatic Constitution on the Church, *Lumen Gentium*, n. 1).

Homily, 18.5.08

19. The Church, the mystical body of Christ

It seems to me that we must interiorise this ecclesiology far more, that of *Lumen Gentium* and of *Ad Gentes*, which is also an ecclesiological Document, as well as the ecclesiology of the minor Documents and of *Dei Verbum*.

By interiorising this vision we can also attract our people to this vision, which understands that the Church is not merely a large structure, one of these supranational bodies that exist. Although she is a body, the Church is the Body of Christ, hence, she is a spiritual body, as St Paul said. She is a spiritual reality. I think this is very important: that people see that the Church is not a supranational organisation nor an administrative body or power, that she is not a social agency, but indeed that although she does social and supranational work, she is a spiritual body.

Speech, 22.2.07

20. The people of God

Thus we see that the two concepts "People of God" and "Body of Christ" complete each other and together form the New Testament concept of Church. And whereas "People of God" expresses the continuity of the Church's history, "Body of Christ" expresses the universality inaugurated in the Cross and in the Lord's Resurrection. For us Christians, therefore, "Body of Christ" is not only an image, but a true concept, because Christ makes us the gift of his real Body, not only an image of it. Risen, Christ unites us all in the Sacrament to make us one Body. Thus the concept "People of God" and "Body of Christ" complete one another: in Christ we really become the People of God. "People of God" therefore means "all", from the Pope to the most recently baptised child....

Subsequent to the Council this ecclesiological doctrine met with acceptance on a vast scale and thanks be to God an abundance of good fruit developed in the Christian community. However, we must also remember that the integration of this doctrine in procedures and its consequent assimilation in the fabric of ecclesial awareness did not happen always and everywhere without difficulty and in accordance with a correct interpretation. As I was able to explain in my Discourse to the Roman Curia on 22 December 2005, an interpretative current, claiming to refer to a presumed "spirit of the Council", sought to establish a discontinuity and even to distinguish between the Church before and the Church after the Council, at times even crossing the very boundaries that exist objectively between the hierarchical ministry and the responsibilities of the lay faithful in the Church. The notion of "People of God", in particular was interpreted by some, in accordance with a purely sociological vision, with an almost exclusively horizontal bias that excluded the vertical reference to God. This position was in direct contrast with the word and spirit of the Council which did not desire a rupture, another Church, but rather a true and deep renewal in the continuity of the one subject-Church which grows in time and develops but always remains identical, the one subject of the People of God on pilgrimage.

Speech, 26.5.09

21. The laity

The Council has offered wise directives so that "the faithful should learn to distinguish carefully between the rights and the duties which they have as belonging to the Church and those which fall to them as members of the human society", and "they will strive to unite the two harmoniously, remembering that in every temporal affair they are to be guided by a Christian conscience, since not even in temporal business may any human activity be withdrawn from God's dominion" (*Lumen Gentium,* n. 36).

For this very reason the Council exhorts lay believers to welcome "what is decided by the Pastors as teachers and rulers of the Church", and then recommends that "Pastors... should recognise and promote the dignity and responsibility of the laity in the Church. They should willingly use their prudent advice" and concludes that "[m]any benefits for the Church are to be expected from this familiar relationship between the laity and the Pastors" (cf. *Lumen Gentium*, n. 37).

Speech, 24.2.07

22. New charisms

In various Documents the Second Vatican Council makes reference to the Movements and new Ecclesial Communities, especially in the Dogmatic Constitution *Lumen Gentium,* where we read: "Whether these charisms be very remarkable or more simple and widely diffused, they are to be received with thanksgiving and consolation" (n. 12). Later the *Catechism of the Catholic Church* also emphasised the value and importance of new charisms in the Church, whose authenticity however is guaranteed by their openness to subject themselves to the discernment of the ecclesiastic authority (cf. n. 2003). Precisely because we are assisting at a promising flowering of Movements and Ecclesial Communities, it is important that Pastors exercise prudent and wise discernment in their regard. I sincerely hope that dialogue between Pastors and Ecclesial Movements intensifies at all levels: parish, diocesan and with the Apostolic See. I know that opportune ways are being studied to give Pontifical recognition to the New Movements and Ecclesial Communities and many have already received it. This fact - the recognition or establishment of international associations on the part of the Holy See for the universal Church - Pastors, especially Bishops, cannot fail to take it into account in their dutiful discernment that lies within their competence (cf. *Apostolorum Successores*, ch. 4, 8).

Speech, 31.10.08

23. The universal vocation to sanctity

The Second Vatican Council highlights the universal call to holiness, when it affirms: "The followers of Christ are called by God, not because of their works, but according to his own purpose and grace. They are justified in the Lord Jesus, because in the Baptism of faith they truly become sons of God and sharers in the divine nature. In this way, they are really made holy" (*Lumen Gentium*, 40). Within the framework of this universal call, Christ, the High Priest, in his solicitude for the Church calls persons in every generation who are to care for his people. In particular, he calls to the ministerial priesthood men who are to exercise a fatherly role, the source of which is within the very fatherhood of God (cf. *Ep* 3:14). The mission of the priest in the Church is irreplaceable.

Message for the 43rd World Day of Prayer for Vocations, 7.5.06

24. Sacrament of salvation

Hence, as the Second Vatican Council expresses it, the Church is the "universal sacrament of salvation" (*Lumen Gentium*, 48), existing for sinners, for us, in order to open up to us the path of conversion, healing and life. That is the Church's great perennial mission, entrusted to her by Christ.

Homily, 22.9.11

25. Mary in the mystery of the church

Between Mary and the Church there is indeed a connatural relationship that was strongly emphasised by the Second Vatican Council in its felicitous decision to place the treatment of the Blessed Virgin at the conclusion of the Constitution on the Church, *Lumen Gentium*.

Homily, 25.3.06

Dei Verbum
(Dogmatic Constitution on Divine Revelation, 18 November 1965)

26. Listening

The Dogmatic Constitution *Dei Verbum*, whose drafting I personally witnessed as a young theologian, taking part in the lively discussions that went with it, begins with a deeply meaningful sentence: "*Dei Verbum religiose audiens et fidenter proclamans, Sacrosancta Synodus...*" ["Hearing the Word of God with reverence, and proclaiming it with faith, the Sacred Synod..."] (n. 1). With these words the Council points out a descriptive aspect of the Church: she is a community that listens to and proclaims the Word of God. The Church does not live on herself but on the Gospel, and in the Gospel always and ever anew finds the directions for her journey. This is a point that every Christian must understand and apply to himself or herself: only those who first listen to the Word can become preachers of it. Indeed, they must not teach their own wisdom but the wisdom of God, which often appears to be foolishness in the eyes of the world (cf. *1 Co* 1:23).

Speech, 16.9.05

27. Pillar

This Document [*Dei Verbum*] is one of the pillars on which the entire Council is built. It addresses Revelation and its transmission, the inspiration and interpretation of Sacred Scripture, and its fundamental importance in the life of the Church. Gathering the fruits of the theological renewal that preceded it, Vatican II put Christ at the centre, presenting him as "both the mediator and the sum total of Revelation" (n. 2). Indeed, the Lord Jesus, the Word made flesh who died and rose, brought to completion the work of salvation, consisting of deeds and words, and fully manifested the face and will of God so that no new public revelation is to be expected until his glorious return (cf. n. 3). The Apostles and their successors, the Bishops, are depositories of the message that Christ entrusted to his Church so that it might be passed on in its integrity to all generations. Sacred Scripture of the Old and New Testaments and sacred Tradition contain this message, whose understanding develops in the Church with the help of the Holy Spirit. This same Tradition makes known the integral canon of the sacred Books. It makes them directly understandable and operative so that God, who has spoken to the Patriarchs and Prophets, does not cease to speak to the Church and, through her, to the world (cf. n. 8).

Angelus, 6.11.05

28. The Apostolic Tradition

This topic of Tradition is so important that I would like to reflect upon it again today: indeed, it is of great importance for the life of the Church. The Second Vatican Council pointed out in this regard that Tradition is primarily *apostolic* in its origins: "God graciously arranged that the things he had once revealed for the salvation of all peoples should remain in their entirety, throughout the ages, and be transmitted to all generations. Therefore, Christ the Lord, in whom the entire Revelation of the Most High God is summed up (cf. *2 Co* 1:20; and 3:16-4,6), commanded the Apostles to preach the Gospel... and communicate the gifts of God to all men. This Gospel was to be the source of all saving truth and moral discipline" (*Dei Verbum*, n. 7). The Council noted further that this was faithfully done "by the Apostles who handed on, by the spoken word of their preaching, by the example they gave, by the institutions they established, what they themselves had received - whether from the lips of Christ, from his way of life and his works, or whether they had learned it at the prompting of the Holy Spirit" (ibid.). The Council adds that there were "other men associated with the Apostles, who, under the inspiration of the same Holy Spirit, committed the message of salvation to writing" (ibid.).

Catechesis, 3.5.06

29. Twofold banquet

This is why "the Church", as the Second Vatican Council highlights, "has always venerated the divine Scriptures as she venerated the Body of the Lord, in so far as she never ceases, particularly in the sacred liturgy, to partake of the bread of life and to offer it to the faithful from the one table of the Word of God and the Body of Christ" (*Dei Verbum*, n. 21). The Council rightly concludes: "Just as persevering devotion to the eucharistic mystery augments the Church's Life, so a new impulse of spiritual life may be expected from increased veneration of the Word of God, which "stands for ever"" (*Dei Verbum*, n. 26). May the Lord grant that we approach with faith the twofold banquet of the Body and Blood of Christ. May Mary Most Holy, who "kept all these things, pondering them in her heart" (*Lk* 2:19) obtain this for us. May she teach us to listen to the Scriptures and meditate upon them in an inner process of maturation that never separates the mind from the heart.

Homily, 5.10.08

30. Biblical exegesis (1)

In particular, the Conciliar Constitution *Dei Verbum* still illumines the work of Catholic exegetes today and invites Pastors and faithful to be more regularly nourished at the table of the Word of God. In this regard the Council recalls first of all that God is the Author of Sacred Scripture: "The divinely revealed realities, which are contained and presented in the text of Sacred Scripture, have been written down under the inspiration of the Holy Spirit. For Holy Mother Church, relying on the faith of the apostolic age, accepts as sacred and canonical the Books of the Old and the New Testaments, whole and entire, with all their parts, on the grounds that, written under the inspiration of the Holy Spirit, they have God as their author, and have been handed on as such to the Church herself" (*Dei Verbum*, n. 11). Therefore since all that the inspired authors or hagiographers state is to be considered as said by the Holy Spirit, the invisible and transcendent Author, it must consequently be acknowledged that "the books of Scripture, firmly, faithfully and without error, teach that truth which God, for the sake of our salvation, wished to see confided to the sacred Scriptures" (ibid., n. 11).

Speech, 23.4.09

31. Biblical exegesis (2)

One aspect very deeply reflected upon was the relationship between the Word and words, that is, between the Divine Word and the Scriptures that express it. As the Second Vatican Council teaches in the Constitution *Dei Verbum* (n. 12), a good biblical exegesis demands both the historical-critical and theological methods since Sacred Scripture is the Word of God in human words. This means that every text must be read and interpreted keeping in mind the unity of the whole of Scripture, the living Tradition of the Church and the light of the faith. If it is true that the Bible is also a literary work, even the great codex of universal culture, it is also true that it should not be stripped of the divine element but must be read in the same Spirit in which it was composed. Scientific exegesis and *lectio divina* are therefore both necessary and complementary in order to seek, through the literal meaning, the spiritual meaning that God wants to communicate to us today.

Angelus, 26.10.08

32. Biblical exegesis (3)

From the correct presentation of the divine inspiration and truth of Sacred Scripture certain norms derive that directly concern its interpretation. The Constitution *Dei Verbum* itself, after stating that God is the author of the Bible, reminds us that in Sacred Scripture God speaks to man in a human fashion and this divine-human synergy is very important:

God really speaks to men and women in a human way. For a correct interpretation of Sacred Scripture it is therefore necessary to seek attentively what the hagiographers have truly wished to state and what it has pleased God to express in human words. "The words of God, expressed in the words of men, are in every way like human language, just as the Word of the eternal Father, when he took on himself the flesh of human weakness, became like men" (*Dei Verbum*, n. 13). Moreover, these indications, very necessary for a correct historical and literary interpretation as the primary dimension of all exegesis, require a connection with the premises of the teaching on the inspiration and truth of Sacred Scripture. In fact, since Scripture is inspired, there is a supreme principal for its correct interpretation without which the sacred writings would remain a dead letter of the past alone: Sacred Scripture "must be read and interpreted with its divine authorship in mind" (ibid., n. 12).…. The scientific study of the sacred texts is important but is not sufficient in itself because it would respect only the human dimension. To respect the coherence of the Church's faith, the Catholic exegete must be attentive to perceiving the Word of God in these texts, within the faith of the Church herself. If this indispensable reference point is missing, the exegetical research would be incomplete, losing sight of its principal goal, and risk being reduced to a purely literary interpretation in which the true Author God no longer appears.

Speech, 23.4.09

33. Theological exegesis

Dei Verbum, n. 12, offers two methodological guidelines for suitable exegetical work. Firstly, it confirms the necessity of using the historical-critical method, of which it briefly describes the essential elements. This necessity is the result of the Christian principle formulated in *Jn* 1:14, "*Verbum caro factum est*". Historical fact is a constituent dimension of the Christian faith. The history of salvation is not mythology but rather true history, and is therefore to be studied alongside serious historical research methods. Nevertheless, this history has another dimension, that of divine action. *Dei Verbum*, consequentially, speaks of a second methodological level necessary for the correct interpretation of the words that are simultaneously human words and the divine Word. … Only where the two methodological levels, both historical-critical and theological, are observed can one speak of theological exegesis, of an exegesis adequate to this Book. While, at the first level, academic exegetical work is currently being done to an extremely high standard and provides us real help, the same cannot be said of the other level. Often this second level … appear[s] almost absent. And this has rather grave consequences. The first consequence of the absence of this second methodological level is that the Bible becomes solely a history book. Moral consequences can be drawn from it, history can be learned from it, but the Book as such speaks of history alone and exegesis is no longer truly theological but instead becomes purely historiographical, literary history. This is the first consequence: the Bible remains in the past, speaks only of the past. The second consequence is even graver: where the hermeneutics of faith explained in *Dei Verbum* disappear, another type of hermeneutics will appear by necessity, a hermeneutics that is secularist, positivist, the key fundamental of which is the conviction that the Divine does not appear in human history.

Speech, 14.10.08

34. A new impulse

We are grateful to God that in recent times, and thanks to the impact made by the Dogmatic Constitution *Dei Verbum*, the fundamental importance of the Word of God has been deeply re-evaluated. From this has derived a renewal of the Church's life, especially in her preaching, catechesis, theology and spirituality, and even in the ecumenical process. The Church must be constantly renewed and rejuvenated and the Word of God, which never ages and is never depleted, is a privileged means to achieve this goal.

Speech, 16.9.05

Gaudium et Spes
**(Pastoral Constitution in the Modern World,
7 December 1965)**

35. The signs of the times

The Second Vatican Council, in the Pastoral Constitution
Gaudium et Spes, also invites believers to examine the
signs of the times in the light of the Gospel, in order to
find in them a manifestation of God's action (cf. nn. 4, 11).
This attitude of faith leads men and women to recognise
the power of God who works in history and thus to open
themselves to feeling awe for the name of the Lord. In
biblical language, in fact, this "fear" is not fright, it does
not denote fear, for fear of God is something quite different.
It is recognition of the mystery of divine transcendence.
Thus, it is at the root of faith and is interwoven with love.
Sacred Scripture says in Deuteronomy: "What does the
Lord, your God, ask of you but to fear the Lord, your God,
and... to love... the Lord, your God, with all your heart and
all your soul" (cf. *Dt* 10:12).

Catechesis, 11.5.05

36. The contemporary world

The contemporary world continues to present
contradictions so clearly outlined by the Fathers of the
Second Vatican Council (cf. *Gaudium et Spes*, nn. 4-10):
we see a humanity that would like to be self-sufficient,

where more than a few consider it almost possible to do without God in order to live well; and yet how many seem sadly condemned to face the dramatic situations of an empty existence, how much violence there still is on the earth, how much solitude weighs on the soul of the humanity of the communications era! In a word, it seems that today there is even loss of the "sense of sin", but in return the "guilt complex" has increased. Who can free the heart of humankind from this yoke of death if not the One who by dying overcame for ever the power of evil with the omnipotence of divine love? As St Paul reminded the Christians of Ephesus: "God, who is rich in mercy, out of the great love with which he loved us, even when we were dead through our trespasses, made us alive together with Christ" (*Ep* 2:4).

Speech, 16.3.07

37. Religious meaning

Modern culture has legitimately emphasised the autonomy of the human person and earthly realities, thereby developing a perspective dear to Christianity, the Incarnation of God. However, as the Second Vatican Council clearly asserted, if this autonomy leads us to think that "material being does not depend on God and that man can use it as if it had no relation to its Creator", a deep imbalance will result, for "without a Creator there can be no creature" (*Gaudium et Spes*, n. 36). It is significant that in the passage cited, the conciliar Document states that this capacity to recognise the voice and manifestation of God in the beauty of creation belongs to all believers, regardless of their religion. From this we can conclude that full respect for life is linked to a *religious sense*, to the inner attitude with which the human being faces reality, as master or as custodian. Moreover, the word "*respect*" derives from the Latin word *respicere*, to look at, and means a way of looking at things and people that leads to recognising their substantial character, not to appropriate them but rather to treat them with respect and to take care of them. In the final analysis, if creatures are deprived of their reference to God as a transcendent basis, they risk being at the mercy of the will of man who, as we see, can make an improper use of it.

Homily, 5.2.06

38. History and createdness

I remember when the conciliar Constitution *Gaudium et Spes* was discussed. On the one hand, there was a recognition of the new, of newness, the "yes" of the Church to the new epoch with its innovations, its "no" to the romanticism of the past, a proper and necessary "no".

However, the Fathers - proof of this is also in the text - also said that in spite of this, in spite of the necessary willingness to move forward and even leave behind other things that were dear to us, there is something that does not change, because it is the human being himself, his state as a creature. Man is not completely historical. The absolutising of historicism, in the sense that man is only and always a creature, the product of a certain period, is not true. His nature as a creature exists, and it is precisely this that gives us the possibility to live through change and to retain our identity.

Speech, 2.3.06

39. The encounter with Jesus

Our answer is the proclamation of God, the friend of man, who through Jesus became close to each one of us. The transmission of the faith is an inalienable part of the integral formation of the person, because in Jesus Christ the hope of a fulfilled life is realised: as the Second Vatican Council teaches, "whoever follows Christ the perfect man becomes himself more a man" (*Gaudium et Spes*, n. 41). The personal encounter with Jesus is the key to understanding the importance of God in our daily existence, the secret of how to live it in brotherly love, the condition that makes it possible to pick ourselves up after a fall and to move towards constant conversion.

Speech, 27.5.10

40. Coherence

In conclusion, to highlight one of the most important aspects of the unity of Christian life, I would like to recall the words of the Pastoral Constitution *Gaudium et Spes*:

consistency between faith and conduct, between Gospel and culture. The Council exhorts the faithful "to perform their duties faithfully in the spirit of the Gospel. It is a mistake to think that, because we have here no lasting city, but seek the city which is to come, we are entitled to shirk our earthly responsibilities; this is to forget that by our faith we are bound all the more to fulfil these responsibilities according to the vocation of each one" (n. 43). In following the Magisterium of St Maximus and of many other Fathers, let us make our own the Council's desire that the faithful may be increasingly anxious to "carry out their earthly activity in such a way as to integrate human, domestic, professional, scientific and technical enterprises with religious values, under whose supreme direction all things are ordered to the glory of God" (ibid.) and thus for humanity's good.

Audience, 31.10.07

41. Culture

The Second Vatican Ecumenical Council paid great attention to culture, and the Pastoral Constitution on the Church in the Modern World *Gaudium et Spes* dedicated a special chapter to it (cf. nn. 53-62). The Council Fathers were concerned to point out the perspective in which the Church views and addresses the promotion of culture, considering this task as one of the "more urgent problems deeply affecting the human race" (ibid., n. 46). In her relations with the world of culture, the Church always places man at the centre, both as the author of cultural activity and the one to whom it is destined.

Speech, 15.5.07

42. Marriage (1)

And Jesus added: "So they are no longer two but one. What therefore God has joined together, let not man put asunder" (*Mk* 10:8-9). This is God's original plan, as the Second Vatican Council also recalled in the Constitution *Gaudium et Spes*: "The intimate partnership of life and love which constitutes the married state has been established by the Creator and endowed by him with its own proper laws: it is rooted in the contract of its partners... God himself is the author of marriage" (n. 48).

Angelus, 8.10.06

43. Marriage (2)

Indeed, it seems to some that the conciliar teaching on marriage, and, in particular, the description of this institution as *"intima communitas vitae et amoris"* [*the intimate partnership of life and love*] (Pastoral Constitution on the Church in the Modern World, *Gaudium et Spes*, n. 48), must lead to a denial of the existence of an indissoluble conjugal bond because this would be a question of an "ideal" to which "normal Christians" cannot be "constrained". In fact, the conviction that the pastoral good of the person in an irregular marital situation requires a sort of canonical regularisation, independently of the validity or nullity of his/her marriage, independently, that is, of the "truth" of his/her personal status, has also spread in certain ecclesiastical milieus.… [M]arriage has a truth of its own - that is, the human knowledge, illumined by the Word of God, of the sexually different reality of the man and of the woman with their profound needs for complementarity, definitive self-giving and exclusivity - to whose discovery and deepening reason and faith harmoniously contribute.

Speech, 27.1.07

44. The truth of peace (1)

The Pastoral Constitution *Gaudium et Spes*, promulgated forty years ago at the conclusion of the Second Vatican Council, stated that mankind will not succeed in "building a truly more human world for everyone, everywhere on earth, unless all people are renewed in spirit and converted to the truth of peace"(*Gaudium et Spes*, n. 77). But what do those words, "the truth of peace", really mean? To respond adequately to this question, we must realise that peace cannot be reduced to the simple absence of armed conflict, but needs to be understood as "the fruit of an order which has been planted in human society by its divine Founder", an order "which must be brought about by humanity in its thirst for ever more perfect justice" (*Gaudium et Spes*, n. 7). As the result of an order planned and willed by the love of God, peace has an intrinsic and invincible truth of its own, and corresponds "to an irrepressible yearning and hope dwelling within us" (Blessed John Paul II, *Message for the 2004 World Day of Peace*, 9).

Message, 1.1.06

45. The truth of peace (2)

Peace! This great, heartfelt aspiration of every man and every woman is built day after day by the contribution of all and by treasuring the wonderful heritage passed down to us by the Second Vatican Council with the Pastoral Constitution *Gaudium et Spes*, which says, among other things, that humanity will not succeed in "the establishment of a truly human world for all men over the entire earth, unless everyone devotes himself to the cause of true peace with renewed vigour" (n. 77). The time in history when the Constitution *Gaudium et Spes* was promulgated, 7 December 1965, was not very different from our time. Then, as unfortunately also in our day and age, tensions of various kinds were looming on the world horizon. In the face of the lasting situations of injustice and violence that continue to oppress various parts of the earth, in the face of those that are emerging as new and more insidious threats to peace - terrorism, nihilism and fanatical fundamentalism - it is becoming more necessary than ever to work together for peace!

Homily, 1.1.06

46. New approaches

In the last part of this conciliar document in which the theme of peace among peoples is also addressed is found a basic expression on which it is good to reflect: "Peace will never be achieved once and for all, but must be built up continually" (n. 78). How true this observation is! Unfortunately, wars and violence never cease and the search for peace is always demanding. In years marked by the danger of possible global conflicts, the Second Vatican Council forcefully denounced the arms race in this text. "The arms race, which quite a few countries have entered, is no infallible way of maintaining real peace", and it immediately adds: "the arms race is one of the greatest curses on the human race and the harm it inflicts on the poor is more than can be endured" (*Gaudium et Spes*, n. 81). The Council Fathers followed this troubled observation by expressing a hope: "New approaches, based on reformed attitudes, will have to be chosen in order to remove this stumbling block, to free the earth from its pressing anxieties, and give back to the world a genuine peace" (ibid.). "New approaches", therefore, "based on reformed attitudes", on the renewal of minds and consciences. Today as then, authentic conversion of hearts represents the right path, the only one that can lead each one of us and all humanity to the hoped-for peace. It is the path indicated by Jesus.

Speech, 28.3.09

47. Alpha and omega

"Christ: Alpha and Omega" is the title of the closing paragraph of Part I of the Pastoral Constitution *Gaudium et Spes* of the Second Vatican Council, promulgated 40 years ago. In that beautiful passage, which borrows some words from the Servant of God Pope Paul VI, we read: "The Lord is the goal of human history, the focal point of the desires of history and civilisation, the centre of mankind, the joy of all hearts and the fulfilment of all aspirations. It is he whom the Father raised from the dead, exalted and placed at his right hand, constituting him judge of the living and the dead. Animated and drawn together in his Spirit we press onwards on our journey towards the consummation of history which fully corresponds to the plan of his love: 'to unite all things in him, things in Heaven and things on earth'" (*Gaudium et Spes*, n. 45). In light of the centrality of Christ, *Gaudium et Spes* interprets the condition of contemporary men and women, their vocation and their dignity, and also the milieus in which they live: the family, culture, the economy, politics, the international community. This is the Church's mission, yesterday, today and for ever: to proclaim and witness to Christ so that the human being, every human being, may totally fulfil his or her vocation.

Angelus, 20.11.05

III. Declarations

Gravissimum Educationis
(Declaration on Christian Education,
28 October 1965)

48. The way of life

The Church has always been dedicated to the education of young people, recognised by the Council as something of "paramount importance" for both the life of men and women and for social progress (cf. *Gravissimum Educationis*, Preface). Today too, in an era of global communication, the Ecclesial Community perceives the importance of an educational system that recognises the primacy of man as a person, open to truth and to good. Parents are the primary and principal educators and are assisted by civil society in accordance with the principle of subsidiarity (cf. ibid., n. 3). The Church, to whom Christ entrusted the duty to proclaim the "way of salvation" (cf. ibid.), feels she has a special educational responsibility. In different ways, she seeks to fulfil this mission: in families, in the parish, through associations, movements and groups of formation and of evangelical commitment and, in a specific way, in schools, institutes of advanced studies and in universities (cf. ibid., nn. 5-12).

Angelus, 30.10.05

Nostra Aetate
(Declaration on the Relation of the Church
to non-Christian Religions, 28 October 1965)

49. Interreligious dialogue

Even the Declaration *Nostra Aetate* is very relevant because it concerns the attitude of the Ecclesial Community in relation to non-Christian religions. Starting with the principle that "all men and women form but one community" and that the Church has the duty "to foster unity and charity" among individuals (n. 1), the Council "rejects nothing of what is true and holy" in other religions and to everyone proclaims Christ, "the way, the truth and the life", in whom men and women find the "fullness of their religious life" (n. 2). With the Declaration *Nostra Aetate* the Fathers of the Second Vatican Council proposed some fundamental truths: they clearly mentioned the special bond that joins Christians to Jews (n. 4); they confirmed their high regard for the Muslims (n. 3) and the followers of other religions (n. 2); and they confirmed the spirit of universal fraternity that rejects any form of discrimination or religious persecution (n. 5).

Angelus, 30.10.05

50. Brothers in God

As the Second Vatican Council taught in the Declaration *Nostra Aetate* on the Relation of the Church to Non-Christian Religions: "We cannot truly pray to God the Father of all if we treat any people in other than brotherly fashion, for all men are created in God's image" (n. 5). Despite the differences that mark the various religious itineraries, recognition of God's existence, which human beings can only arrive at by starting from the experience of creation (cf. *Rm* 1:20), must dispose believers to view other human beings as brothers and sisters. It is not legitimate, therefore, for anyone to espouse religious difference as a presupposition or pretext for an aggressive attitude towards other human beings.

Message, 2.9.06

51. A common path

The Second Vatican Council affirms that "All peoples are one community and have one origin, because God caused the whole human race to dwell on the face of the earth (cf. *Ac* 17:26); they also have one final end, God" (*Message for the World Day of Peace*, 2008, 1). "His providence, His manifestations of goodness, His saving design extend to all men" (Declaration *Nostra Aetate*, 1). Thus, "We do not live alongside one another purely by chance; all of us are progressing along a common path as men and women, and thus as brothers and sisters" (*Message for the World Day of Peace*, 2008, 6).

Message, 27.9.10

52. The Church's missionary task

[C]onfronted by the risk of persistent religious and cultural relativism, [it is] reaffirm[ed] that in the age of interreligious and intercultural dialogue the Church does not dispense with the need for evangelisation and missionary activity for peoples, nor does she cease to ask men and women to accept the salvation offered to them all. Recognition of elements of truth and good in the world's religions and the seriousness of their religious endeavours, together with dialogue and a spirit of collaboration with them for the defence and promotion of dignity and universal moral values, cannot be understood as a limitation of the Church's missionary task, which involves her in ceaselessly proclaiming Christ as the Way, the Truth and the Life (cf. *Jn* 14:6).

Dignitatis Humanae
(Declaration on Religious Freedom, 7 December 1965)

53. The search for truth

In particular, the Council Fathers approved, precisely 40 years ago, a Declaration on the question of religious liberty, that is, the right of persons and of communities to seek the truth and to profess their faith freely. The first words that give this document its title are "*dignitatis humanae*": religious liberty derives from the special dignity of the human person, who is the only one of all the creatures on this earth who can establish a free and conscious relationship with his or her Creator.

"It is in accordance with their dignity that all men, because they are persons, that is, beings endowed with reason and free will..., are both impelled by their nature and bound by a moral obligation to seek the truth, especially religious truth" (*Dignitatis Humanae*, n. 2).

Thus, the Second Vatican Council reaffirms the traditional Catholic doctrine which holds that men and women, as spiritual creatures, can know the truth and therefore have the duty and the right to seek it (cf. ibid., n. 3).

Having laid this foundation, the Council places a broad emphasis on religious liberty, which must be guaranteed both to individuals and to communities with respect for the legitimate demands of public order. And after 40 years, this conciliar teaching is still most timely.

Religious liberty is indeed very far from being effectively guaranteed everywhere: in certain cases it is denied for religious or ideological reasons; at other times, although it may be recognisable on paper, it is hindered in effect by political power or, more cunningly, by the cultural predomination of agnosticism and relativism.

Angelus, 4.12.05

IV. Decrees

Inter Mirifica
(Decree on the Media of Social Communications, 4 December 1965)

54. The media

Knowledge of the value and great usefulness of the media for disseminating the Gospel and forming consciences has grown since the Second Vatican Council.

Speech, 1.10.05

55. Networks

In the wake of the fortieth anniversary of the closing of the Second Vatican Ecumenical Council, I am happy to recall its Decree on the Means of Social Communication, *Inter Mirifica*, which in particular recognised the power of the media to influence the whole of human society [and] the need to harness that power for the benefit of all mankind....

Message, 24.1.06

56. New media

The human being, therefore, does not only "use" but, in a certain sense, "dwells" in language. Today, in particular, what the Second Vatican Council described as "marvellous technical inventions" (*Inter Mirifica*, n. 1) are transforming the cultural environment and this requires specific attention to the languages that are developing in it. The power of the new technologies "extends to defining not only what people will think but even what they will think about" (*Aetatis Novae*, n. 4).

Speech, 28.2.11

Unitatis Redintegratio
(Decree on Ecumenism, 21 November 1965)

57. Spiritual ecumenism

I mentioned just now that the Second Vatican Council paid great attention to the topic of Christian unity, especially in the Decree on Ecumenism (*Unitatis Redintegratio*), in which, among other things, the role and importance of prayer for unity is forcefully emphasised. Prayer, the Council observed, is at the very heart of the entire ecumenical process. "This change of heart and holiness of life, along with public and private prayer for the unity of Christians, should be regarded as the soul of the whole ecumenical movement" (*Unitatis Redintegratio*, n. 8). Thanks precisely to this spiritual ecumenism - holiness of life, conversion of heart, private and public prayer - the common search for unity has in recent decades recorded considerable development. This has been diversified in multiple initiatives: from mutual knowledge to brotherly contact between the members of different Churches and Ecclesial Communities, from ever more friendly conversations to collaboration in various fields, from theological dialogue to the search for concrete forms of communion and collaboration.

Catechesis, 23.1.08

58. Common prayer (1)

Prayer for unity is part of the central nucleus which the Second Vatican Council calls "the soul of the whole ecumenical movement" (*Unitatis Redintegratio*, n. 8), a nucleus that includes public and private prayers, conversion of heart and holiness of life. This vision takes us back to the heart of the ecumenical problem, which is obedience to the Gospel in order to do God's will with his necessary and effective help. The Council explicitly pointed this out to the faithful, declaring: "The closer their union with the Father, the Word, and the Spirit, the more deeply and easily will they be able to grow in mutual brotherly love" (ibid., n. 7).

The elements that, despite the persistent division, still unite Christians, make it possible to raise a common prayer to God. This communion in Christ sustains the entire ecumenical movement and indicates the very purpose of the search for unity of all Christians in God's Church. It is what distinguishes the ecumenical movement from any other initiative of dialogue and relations with other religions and ideologies.

Catechesis, 18.1.06

59. Common prayer (2)

[T]he Council places the emphasis on prayer in common, prayer raised jointly to the one Heavenly Father by Catholics and by other Christians. The Decree on Ecumenism says in this regard: "Such prayers in common are certainly a very effective means of petitioning for the grace of unity" (*Unitatis Redintegratio*, n. 8). And this is because, in praying together, Christian communities place themselves before the Lord and, becoming aware of the contradictions to which division has given rise, manifest their desire to obey the Lord's will with trusting recourse to his almighty assistance. The Decree then adds that such prayers "are a genuine expression of the ties which still bind Catholics to their separated (*seiuncti*) brethren" (ibid.). Prayer in common is not, therefore, a voluntaristic or purely sociological act, but rather an expression of faith that unites all Christ's disciples.

Catechesis, 23.1.08

60. Interior conversion

[In the Decree *Unitatis Redintegratio*] among other things, one reads: "There can be no ecumenism worthy of the name without interior conversion. For it is from newness of attitudes of mind (cf. *Ep* 4:23), from self-denial and unstinted love, that desires of unity take their rise and develop in a mature way" (n. 7). The attitude of interior conversion in Christ, of spiritual renewal, of growth in charity towards other Christians has given way to a new situation in ecumenical relations. The fruits of theological dialogue, with their convergence and with the most precise identification of the divergences that still remain, urge the courageous pursuance of two directions: in the acceptance of what has been positively achieved and in a renewed commitment towards the future.

Homily, 25.1.09

61. Full unity

The horizon of full unity remains open before us. It is an arduous duty, but stirring for Christians who want to live in harmony with the Lord's prayer: "that they may be one, that the world may believe" (*Jn* 17:21). The Second Vatican Council has given us the prospect of "this holy objective, the reconciliation of all Christians in the unity of the one and only Church of Christ, transcends human powers and gifts" (*Unitatis Redintegratio*, 24). Trusting in the prayer of the Lord Jesus Christ, and encouraged by the significant steps accomplished by the ecumenical movement, let us invoke the Holy Spirit with faith so that he continues to illuminate and guide our way. May the Apostle Paul, who fatigued and suffered so much for the unity of the Mystical Body of Christ, urge us and assist us from heaven.

Homily, 25.1.09

Orientalium Ecclesiarum
**(Decree on the Catholic Churches of the Eastern Rite,
21 November 1965)**

62. Ecumenical horizon

For my part, I feel it is my main duty to encourage the synodality so dear to Eastern ecclesiology and acknowledged with appreciation by the Second Vatican Ecumenical Council. I fully share in the esteem that the Council showed your Churches in the Decree *Orientalium Ecclesiarum* which my venerable predecessor John Paul II reaffirmed in particular in his Apostolic Exhortation *Orientale Lumen*. I also share in the hope that the Eastern Catholic Churches will "flourish" in order "to fulfil with new apostolic strength the task entrusted to them", so as to foster "the unity of all Christians, in particular of Eastern Christians, according to the principles laid down in the decree of this holy Council on ecumenism" (*Orientalium Ecclesiarum*, nn. 1, 24). The ecumenical horizon is often connected with the interreligious outlook. In these two areas the whole Church needs the experience of coexistence, which your Churches have developed since the first Christian millennium.

Speech, 19.9.09

63. Authentic communion

The Second Vatican Council committed the Catholic Church "irrevocably to following the path of the ecumenical venture, thus heeding the Spirit of the Lord who teaches us to interpret carefully the 'signs of the times'" (*Ut Unum Sint*, 3). This is the path that the Catholic Church has wholeheartedly embraced since that time. The Churches of East and West, ... share a real, if still imperfect, communion.

Speech, 18.1.10

Optatam Totius
(Decree on Priestly Training, 28 October 1965)

64. Witness

The Second Vatican Council, in speaking of the witness that awakens vocations, emphasises the example of charity and of fraternal cooperation which priests must offer (cf. *Optatam Totius*, 2).

Message, 25.4.10

Perfectae Caritatis
(Decree on the Adaptation and Renewal
of Religious Life, 28 October 1965)

65. Sequela Christi

[Remembering] the promulgation of the conciliar Decree *Perfectae Caritatis* on the renewal of religious life ... I hope that the fundamental guidelines offered by the Council

Fathers at that time for the progress of the consecrated life will also be a source of inspiration today for all who dedicate their lives to the service of the Kingdom of God.

I am referring primarily to what *Perfectae Caritatis* describes as "vitae religiosae ultima norma", "the final norm of the religious life", that is, the "sequela Christi". A genuine recovery of religious life is impossible without seeking to live in complete conformity with the Gospel, without putting anything before the one Love, but finding in Christ and in his words the essence that is deeper than any Founder's or Foundress's charism.

Letter, 27.9.05

Christus Dominus
(Decree Concerning the Pastoral Office of Bishops in the Church, 28 October 1965)

66. Union

In fact, "Bishops, as legitimate successors of the Apostles and members of the Episcopal College, should appreciate that they are closely united to each other and should be solicitous for all the Churches" (*Christus Dominus*, n. 6). Yet experience tells us that this unity is never achieved once and for all and that it must be ceaselessly built up and perfected, without surrendering to the objective and subjective difficulties but rather with the determination to reveal the Catholic Church's one and only true face.

Speech, 18.5.09

67. Be solicitous

This spirit of communion has a privileged application in the Bishop's relationship with his priests. I am well acquainted with your desire to pay greater attention to your priests, and, in line with the Second Vatican Council, I encourage you to be solicitous, showing fatherly and brotherly love, "for the welfare, spiritual, intellectual, and material, of your priests, so that they may live holy and pious lives, and exercise a faithful and fruitful ministry" (*Christus Dominus*, n. 16). Likewise, I urge you to show charity and caution when you have to correct teachings, attitudes or forms of behaviour that do not befit the priestly condition of your closest collaborators and, moreover, could damage and confuse the faith and the Christian life of the faithful.

Speech, 14.3.09

Apostolicam Actuositatem
(Decree on the Apostolate of the Laity, 18 November 1965)

68. Faithful lay people

On 18 November 1965 the Fathers approved a specific Decree on the Apostolate of Lay People, *Apostolicam Actuositatem*. It stressed first of all that "the fruitfulness of the apostolate of lay people depends on their living union with Christ" (n. 4), that is, on a vigorous spirituality nourished by active participation in the Liturgy and expressed in the style of the Gospel Beatitudes.

For lay people, moreover, professional competence, a sense of family, a civic sense and the social virtues are of great importance. Although it is true that they are called individually to bear their personal witness, particularly precious wherever the freedom of the Church encounters obstacles, the Council nonetheless insisted on the importance of the organised apostolate, essential if an effect is to be made on the general mindset, social conditions and institutions (cf. ibid., n. 18).

Angelus, 13.1.05

69. Apostolate

Yet the Second Vatican Council's vision is that wherever the lay faithful live out their baptismal vocation – in the family, at home, at work - they are actively participating in the Church's mission to sanctify the world. A renewed focus on lay apostolate will help to clarify the roles of clergy and laity and so give a strong impetus to the task of evangelising society.

Speech, 5.2.10

70. Lay realities

The Ecclesial Movements and New Communities are one of the most important innovations inspired by the Holy Spirit in the Church for the implementation of the Second Vatican Council. They spread in the wake of the Council sessions, especially in the years that immediately followed it, in a period full of exciting promises but also marked by difficult trials. ... Indeed, even then [the new lay realities] were already bearing witness to the joy, reasonableness and beauty of being Christian, showing that they were grateful for belonging to the mystery of communion which is the Church. We have witnessed the reawakening of a vigorous missionary impetus, motivated by the desire to communicate to all the precious experience of the encounter with Christ, felt and lived as the only adequate response to the human heart's profound thirst for truth and happiness.

Speech, 17.5.08

Ad Gentes
(Decree on the Mission Activity of the Church, 7 December 1965)

71. The ways of the Holy Spirit

Many [are the] ways inspired by the Holy Spirit with the Second Vatican Council for the new evangelisation.

Speech, 10.1.09

72. The mission

The Church is by nature missionary; her urgent duty is to evangelise. The Second Vatican Council dedicated to missionary activity the Decree entitled, precisely, "*Ad Gentes*". It recalls that "the Apostles... following the footsteps of Christ, 'preached the word of truth and begot churches' (St Augustine, *Enarr. in Ps.* 44, 23: *PL* 36, 508; *CChr.* 30, 510)", and that it "is the duty of their successors to carry on this work so that 'the Word of God may run and be glorified' (*2 The* 3:1) and the Kingdom of God proclaimed and renewed throughout the whole world" (*Ad Gentes*, n.1).

Homily, 25.4.05

Presbyterorum Ordinis
(Decree on the Ministry of the Life of Priests, 7 December 1965)

73. Ecclesial communion

Harvesting the pastoral experience of past centuries, the Second Vatican Council highlighted the importance of educating future priests to an authentic ecclesial communion. In this regard, we read in *Presbyterorum Ordinis*: "Exercising the office of Christ, the shepherd and head, according to their share of his authority, the priests, in the name of the Bishop, gather the family of God together as a brotherhood enlivened by one spirit. Through Christ they lead them in the Holy Spirit to God the Father" (n. 6).... It is indispensable that, within the Christian people, every ministry and charism be directed to full communion; and it is the duty of the Bishop and priests to promote this communion in harmony with every other Church vocation and service.

Message, 10.2.07

74. Co-responsibility

I believe that this is one of the important and positive results of the Council: the co-responsibility of the entire parish, for the parish priest is no longer the only one to animate everything. Since we all form a parish together, we must all collaborate and help so that the parish priest is not left on his own, mainly as a coordinator, but truly discovers that he is a pastor who is backed up in these common tasks in which, together, the parish lives and is fulfilled. Thus, I would say that, on the one hand, this coordination and vital responsibility for the whole parish, and on the other, the sacramental life and preaching as a centre of parish life, could also today, in circumstances which are of course more difficult, make it possible to be a parish priest who may not know each person by name, as the Lord says of the Good Shepherd, but one who really knows his sheep and is really their pastor who calls and guides them.

Speech, 24.7.07

75. Priestly continuity

Just as the hermeneutics of continuity are proving ever more urgent for a satisfactory understanding of the Second Vatican Council's texts, likewise a hermeneutic we might describe as "of priestly continuity" appears necessary. This has come down to our day, starting from Jesus of Nazareth, Lord and Christ, and passing through the 2,000 years of the history of greatness and holiness, of culture and devotion which the Priesthood has written in the world.

Speech, 12.3.10

76. Reception

It is important to encourage in priests, especially in the young generations, a correct reception of the texts of the Second Ecumenical Vatican Council, interpreted in the light of the Church's entire fund of doctrine.

Speech, 16.3.09

V. The Council's Messages

77. "To Rulers" and, the second, "To Men of Thought and Science"

Let us return to that special moment of grace, the conclusion of the Second Vatican Council on 8 December 1965, when the Council Fathers addressed certain "Messages" to all humanity.

The first was addressed "To Rulers" and the second, "To Men of Thought and Science". These are two categories of people who, in a certain way, we can see portrayed in the evangelical figures of the Magi.

I would then like to add a third category, to which the Council did not address a message but which was very present in its attention in the Conciliar Decree *Nostra Aetate*. I am referring to the spiritual leaders of the great non-Christian religions. ... Today, I would like to make my own those Messages of the Council which have lost nothing of their timeliness. For instance, one reads in the Message addressed to Rulers: "Your task is to be in the world the promoters of order and peace among men. But never forget this: It is God, the living and true God, who is the Father of men. And it is Christ, his eternal Son, who came to make this known to us and to teach us that we are all brothers. He it is who is the great artisan of order and peace on earth, for he it is who guides human history and who alone can incline hearts to renounce those evil passions which beget war and misfortune".

How can we fail to recognise in these words of the Council Fathers the luminous trail of a journey which alone can transform the history of the nations and the world?

And further, in the "Message to Men of Thought and Science" we read: "Continue your search without tiring and without ever despairing of the truth"; and this, in fact, is the great danger: losing interest in the truth and seeking only action, efficiency and pragmatism! "Recall the words of one of your great friends, St Augustine: 'Let us seek with the desire to find, and find with the desire to seek still more'. Happy are those who, while possessing the truth, search more earnestly for it in order to renew it, deepen it and transmit it to others. Happy also are those who, not having found it, are working toward it with a sincere heart. May they seek the light of tomorrow with the light of today until they reach the fullness of light".

This was said in these two Council Messages. Today, it is more necessary than ever to flank the leaders of nations and researchers and scientists with the leaders of the great non-Christian religious traditions, inviting them to face one another with the light of Christ, who came not to abolish but to bring to fulfilment what God's hand has written in the religious history of civilisation, especially in the "great souls" who helped to build up humanity with their wisdom and example of virtue.

Christ is light, and light cannot darken but can only illuminate, brighten, reveal.

Homily, 6.1.07

78. The Poor, the Sick, and the Suffering

The Second Ecumenical Vatican Council had already recalled the Church's important task of caring for human suffering. In the Dogmatic Constitution *Lumen Gentium* we read that "Christ was sent by the Father 'to bring good news to the poor... to heal the contrite of heart' (*Lk* 4:18), 'to seek and to save what was lost' (*Lk* 19:10).... Similarly, the Church encompasses with her love all those who are afflicted by human misery and she recognises in those who are poor and who suffer, the image of her poor and suffering Founder. She does all in her power to relieve their need and in them she strives to serve Christ" (n. 8)....

And I am anxious to add that at this moment in history and culture we are feeling even more acutely the need for an attentive and far-reaching ecclesial presence beside the sick, as well as a presence in society that can effectively pass on the Gospel values that safeguard human life in all its phases, from its conception to its natural end.

I would like here to take up the Message to the Poor, the Sick, and the Suffering which the Council Fathers addressed to the world at the end of the Second Ecumenical

Vatican Council: "All of you who feel heavily the weight of the Cross" they said, "you who weep... you the unknown victims of suffering, take courage. You are the preferred children of the Kingdom of God, the Kingdom of hope, happiness, and life. You are the brothers of the suffering Christ, and with him, if you wish, you are saving the world" (Paul VI, *Message*, 8.XII.65).

Message, 22.11.09

Analytical index